Grimm Tales Made Gay

Guy Wetmore Carryl

Illustrated by Albert Levering

GRIMM TALES MADE GAY

BY GUY WETMORE CARRYL

With GAY PICTURES
BY ALBERT LEVERING

GRIMM TALES
MADE GAY
By Guy Wetmore Carryl

With GAY PICTURES
By Albert Levering

This shows the sword that Blue-Beard used full sore,
After he'd led his young wife to a door.

GRIMM TALES MADE GAY

By GUY WETMORE CARRYL

AUTHOR OF

THIS .... AND MANY ···· OTHER ······ THINGS!

PICTURES BY

ALBERT LEVERING

ARTIST OF

THAT   THE OTHER   AND THIS

BOSTON & NEW YORK
HOUGHTON, MIFFLIN & CO.

GRIMM TALES
MADE GAY
By Guy Wetmore Carryl

AUTHOR OF
THIS ...... AND MANY ...... OTHER ...... THINGS!

PICTURES BY
ALBERT LEVERING

ARTIST OF
THAT ...... THE OTHER ...... AND THIS

BOSTON & NEW YORK
HOUGHTON, MIFFLIN & CO.

Published in October, 1902

TO
CHARLES
WALTON
OGDEN

NOTE

I have pleasure in acknowledging the courteous permission of the editors to reprint in this form such of these verses as were originally published in Harper's Magazine, The Century, Life, The Smart Set, The Saturday Evening Post, The Home Magazine, and the London Tatler.
G. W. C.

The Contents

How the Babes in the Wood showed they couldn't be
  beaten

  How Fair Cinderella disposed of her Shoe

How Little Red Riding Hood came to be eaten

  How the Fatuous Wish of a Peasant came True

How Hop o' My Thumb got rid of an Onus

  How the Helpmate of Blue-Beard made free with a
  Door

How Rumplestilz held out in vain for a Bonus

  How Jack made the Giants uncommonly Sore

How Rudeness and Kindness were justly rewarded

  How Beauty contrived to get Square with the Beast

How a Fair One no Hope to his Highness accorded

  How Thomas a Maid from a Dragon released

How a Beauty was waked and her Suitor was suited

  How Jack found that Beans may go back on a Chap

How a Cat was annoyed and a Poet was booted

  How much Fortunatus could do with a Cap

How a Princess was wooed from Habitual Sadness

  How a Girl was too Reckless of Grammar by far

How the Peaceful Aladdin gave Way to his Madness

  How a Fisherman corked up his Foe in a Jar

How the Babes in the Wood
Showed They Couldn't be
Beaten

A man of kind and noble mind
   Was H. Gustavus Hyde.
'Twould be amiss to add to this
   At present, for he died,
In full possession of his senses,
The day before my tale commences.

One half his gold his four-year-old
   Son Paul was known to win,
And Beatrix, whose age was six,
   For all the rest came in,
Perceiving which, their Uncle Ben did
A thing that people said was splendid.

For by the hand he took them, and
　　Remarked in accents smooth:
"One thing I ask. Be mine the task
　　These stricken babes to soothe!
My country home is really charming:
I'll teach them all the joys of farming."

One halcyon week they fished his creek,
　　And watched him do the chores,
In haylofts hid, and, shouting, slid
　　Down sloping cellar doors:—
Because this life to bliss was equal
The more distressing is the sequel.

Concealing guile beneath a smile,
   He took them to a wood,
And, with severe and most austere
   Injunctions to be good,
He left them seated on a gateway,
And took his own departure straightway.

Though much afraid, the children stayed
   From ten till nearly eight;
At times they wept, at times they slept,
   But never left the gate:
Until the swift suspicion crossed them
That Uncle Benjamin had lost them.

Then, quite unnerved, young Paul observed:
   "It's like a dreadful dream,
And Uncle Ben has fallen ten
   Per cent. in my esteem.
Not only did he first usurp us,
But now he's left us here on purpose!"
              *****

For countless years their childish fears
    Have made the reader pale,
For countless years the public's tears
    Have started at the tale,
For countless years much detestation
Has been expressed for their relation.

Grimm Tales Made Gay

So draw a veil across the dale
   Where stood that ghastly gate.
No need to tell. You know full well
   What was their touching fate,
And how with leaves each little dead breast
Was covered by a Robin Redbreast!

But when they found them on the ground,
   Although their life had ceased,
Quite near to Paul there lay a small
   White paper, neatly creased.
"Because of lack of any merit,
B. Hyde," it ran, *"we disinherit!"*

The Moral: If you deeply long
To punish one who's done you wrong,
Though in your lifetime fail you may,
Where there's a will, there is a way!

*How Fair Cinderella Disposed
of Her Shoe*

The vainest girls in forty states
Were Gwendolyn and Gladys Gates;
They warbled, slightly off the air,
  Romantic German songs,
And each of them upon her hair
  Employed the curling tongs,
And each with ardor most intense
Her buxom figure laced,

Until her wilful want of sense
  Procured a woeful waist:
For bound to marry titled mates
Were Gwendolyn and Gladys Gates.

Yet, truth to tell, the swains were few
Of Gwendolyn (and Gladys, too).
So morning, afternoon, and night
  Upon their sister they
Were wont to vent their selfish spite,
  And in the rudest way:
For though her name was Leonore,
  That's neither there nor here,
They called her Cinderella, for
  The kitchen was her sphere,
Save when the hair she had to do
Of Gwendolyn (and Gladys, too).

Each night to dances and to *fêtes*
Went Gwendolyn and Gladys Gates,
And Cinderella watched them go
    In silks and satins clad:
A prince invited them, and so
    They put on all they had!
But one fine night, as all alone
    She watched the flames leap higher,
A small and stooping fairy crone
    Stept nimbly from the fire.
Said she: "The pride upon me grates
Of Gwendolyn and Gladys Gates."
["I'll now," she added, with a frown,
"Call Gwendolyn and Gladys down!"

And, ere your fingers you could snap,
   There stood before the door
No paltry hired horse and trap,
   Oh, no!—a coach and four!
And Cinderella, fitted out
   Regardless of expense,
Made both her sisters look about
   Like thirty-seven cents!
The prince, with one look at her gown,
Turned Gwendolyn and Gladys down!

Wall-flowers, when thus compared with her,
Both Gwendolyn and Gladys were.
The prince but gave them glances hard,
   No gracious word he said;
He scratched their names from off his card,
   And wrote hers down instead:
And where he would bestow his hand
   He showed them in a trice
By handing her the kisses, and
   To each of them an ice!
In sudden need of fire and fur
Both Gwendolyn and Gladys were.

At ten o'clock, in discontent,
Both Gwendolyn and Gladys went.
Their sister stayed till after two,
    And, with a joy sincere,
The prince obtained her crystal shoe
    By way of souvenir.
"Upon the bridal path," he cried,
    "We'll reign together! Since
I love you, you must be my bride!"
    (He was no slouch, that prince!)
And into sudden languishment
Both Gwendolyn and Gladys went.

The Moral: All the girls on earth
Exaggerate their proper worth.

They think the very shoes they wear
Are worth the average millionaire;
Whereas few pairs in any town
Can be half-sold for half a crown!

How Little Red Riding Hood
Came to be Eaten

Most worthy of praise
Were the virtuous ways
  Of Little Red Riding Hood's Ma,
And no one was ever
More cautious and clever
  Than Little Red Riding Hood's Pa.
They never misled,
For they meant what they said,
  And would frequently say what they meant,
And the way she should go
They were careful to show,
  And the way that they showed her, she went.

For obedience she was effusively thanked,

And for anything else she was carefully spanked.

It thus isn't strange
That Red Riding Hood's range
    Of virtues so steadily grew,
That soon she won prizes
Of different sizes,
    And golden encomiums, too!
As a general rule
She was head of her school,
    And at six was so notably smart
That they gave her a cheque
For reciting "The Wreck
    Of the Hesperus," wholly by heart!
And you all will applaud her the more, I am sure,
When I add that this money she gave to the poor.

At eleven this lass
Had a Sunday-school class,
    At twelve wrote a volume of verse,
At thirteen was yearning

For glory, and learning
  To be a professional nurse.
To a glorious height
The young paragon might
  Have grown, if not nipped in the bud,
But the following year
Struck her smiling career
  With a dull and a sickening thud!

(I have shed a great tear at the thought of her pain,
  And must copy my manuscript over again!)

 Not dreaming of harm,
One day on her arm
  A basket she hung. It was filled
With jellies, and ices,
And gruel, and spices,
  And chicken-legs, carefully grilled,
And a savory stew,

And a novel or two
  She'd persuaded a neighbor to loan,
And a hot-water can,

And a Japanese fan,
 And a bottle of *eau-de-cologne,*
And the rest of the things that your family fill
Your room with, whenever you chance to be ill!

She expected to find
Her decrepit but kind
 Old Grandmother waiting her call,
But the visage that met her
Completely upset her:
 It wasn't familiar at all!
With a whitening cheek
She started to speak,
 But her peril she instantly saw:—
Her Grandma had fled,
And she'd tackled instead
 Four merciless Paws and a Maw!
When the neighbors came running, the wolf to subdue,
He was licking his chops, (and Red Riding Hood's, too!)

At this terrible tale
Some readers will pale,
 And others with horror grow dumb,
And yet it was better,
I fear, he should get her:
 Just think what she might have become!
For an infant so keen
Might in future have been
 A woman of awful renown,
Who carried on fights
For her feminine rights
 As the Mare of an Arkansas town.
She might have continued the crime of her 'teens,
And come to write verse for the Big Magazines!

This shows the bad wolf that came out of the wood,
And proved by his actions to be robbin' Hood.

The Moral: There's nothing much glummer
   Than children whose talents appall:
One much prefers those who are dumber,
   But as for the paragons small,
If a swallow cannot make a summer
   It can bring on a summary fall!

How the Fatuous Wish of a
Peasant Came True

An excellent peasant,
Of character pleasant,
  Once lived in a hut with his wife.
He was cheerful and docile,
But such an old fossil
  You wouldn't meet twice in your life.
His notions were all without reason or rhyme,
Such dullness in any one else were a crime,
  But the folly pig-headed
To which he was wedded
Was so deep imbedded,
  it touched the sublime!

He frequently stated
Such quite antiquated
  And singular doctrines as these:
"Do good unto others!
All men are your brothers!"
  (Of course he forgot the Chinese!)
He said that all men were made equal and free,
(That's true if they're born on *our* side of the sea!)
  That truth should be spoken,
And pledges unbroken:
(Now where, by that token,
would most of us be?)

One day, as his pottage
He ate in his cottage,
  A fairy stepped up to the door;
Upon it she hammered,
And meekly she stammered:
  "A morsel of food I implore."
He gave her sardines, and a biscuit or two,
And she said in reply, when her luncheon was
      through,
  "In return for these dishes
Of bread and of fishes
The first of your wishes
  I'll make to come true!"
That nincompoop peasant

Accepted the present,
  (As most of us probably would,)
And, thinking her bounty
To turn to account, he
  Said: "*Now* I'll do somebody good!
I won't ask a thing for myself or my wife,
But I'll make all my neighbors with happiness rife.
  Whate'er their conditions,
  Henceforward, physicians
  And indispositions
      they're rid of for life!"

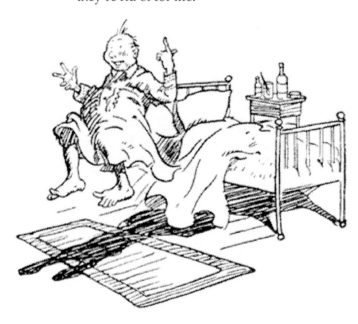

These words energetic
The fairy's prophetic
  Announcement brought instantly true:
With singular quickness
Each victim of sickness
  Was made over, better than new,
And people who formerly thought they were
      doomed

With almost obstreperous healthiness bloomed,
    And each had some platitude,
    Teeming with gratitude,
    For the new attitude
        life had assumed.

Our friend's satisfaction
Concerning his action
    Was keen, but exceedingly brief.
The wrathful condition
Of every physician
    In town was surpassing belief!
Professional nurses were plunged in despair,
And chemists shook passionate fists in the air:
    They called at his dwelling,
    With violence swelling,
His greeting repelling
        with arrogant stare.

They beat and they battered,
They slammed and they shattered,
   And did him such serious harm,
That, after their labors,
His wife told the neighbors
   They'd caused her excessive alarm!
They then set to work on his various ills,
And plied him with liniments, powders, and pills,
   And charged him so dearly
   That all of them nearly
   Made double the yearly
      amount of their bills.

This Moral by the tale is taught: —
The wish is father to the thought.
(We'd oftentimes escape the worst
If but the thinking part came first!)

How Hop O' My Thumb Got
Rid of an Onus

A worthy couple, man and wife,
Dragged on a discontented life:
   The reason, I should state,
That it was destitute of joys,
Was that they had a dozen boys
   To feed and educate,
And nothing such patience demands
As having twelve boys on your hands!

For twenty years they tried their best
To keep those urchins neatly dressed
   And teach them to be good,
But so much labor it involved

23

That, in the end, they both resolved
　　To lose them in a wood,
Though nothing a parent annoys
Like heartlessly losing his boys!

So when their sons had gone to bed,
Though bitter tears the couple shed,
　　They laid their little plan.
"*Faut b'en que ça s'fasse. Quand même,*"
The woman said, "*J'en suis tout' blème.*"
　　"*Ça colle!*" observed the man,
"*Mais ça coute, que ces gosses fichus!
B'en, quoi! Faut qu'i's soient perdus!*"

(I've quite omitted to explain
That they were natives of Touraine;
　　I see I must translate.)
"Of course it must be done, and still,"
The wife remarked, "it makes me ill."
　　"You bet!" replied her mate:
"But we've both of us counted the cost,
And the kids simply *have* to be lost!"

But, while they plotted, every word
The youngest of the urchins heard,
   And winked the other eye;
His height was only two feet three.
(I might remark, in passing, he
   Was little, but O My!)
He added: "I'd better keep mum."
(He was foxy, was Hop O' My Thumb!)

They took the boys into the wood,
And lost them, as they said they should,
   And came in silence back.
Alas for them! Hop O' My Thumb
At every step had dropped a crumb,
   And so retraced the track.
While the parents sat mourning their fate
He led the boys in at the gate!

He placed his hand upon his heart,
And said: "You think you're awful smart,
   But I have foiled you thus!"
His parents humbly bent the knee,
And meekly said: "H. O. M. T.,
   You're one too much for us!"
And both of them solemnly swore
"We won't never do so no more!"

The Moral is: While I do not
Endeavor to condone the plot,
   I still maintain that one
Should have no chance of being foiled,
And having one's arrangements spoiled
   By one's ingenious son.
If you turn down your children, with pain,
Take care they don't turn up again!

How the Helpmate of Blue-Beard
Made Free with a Door

A maiden from the Bosphorus,
With eyes as bright as phosphorus,
Once wed the wealthy bailiff
    Of the caliph
        Of Kelat.

Though diligent and zealous, he
Became a slave to jealousy.
  (Considering her beauty,
    'Twas his duty
      To be that!)

When business would necessitate
A journey, he would hesitate,
  But, fearing to disgust her,
    He would trust her
      With his keys,
Remarking to her prayerfully:
"I beg you'll use them carefully.
  Don't look what I deposit
    In that closet,
      If you please."

It may be mentioned, casually,
That blue as lapis lazuli
  He dyed his hair, his lashes,
    His mustaches,
      And his beard.
And, just because he did it, he
Aroused his wife's timidity:
  Her terror she dissembled,
    But she trembled
      When he neared.

This feeling insalubrious
Soon made her most lugubrious,
  And bitterly she missed her
    Elder sister
    Marie Anne:
She asked if she might write her to
Come down and spend a night or two,
  Her husband answered rightly
    And politely:
      "Yes, you can!"

This shows how grim Blue-Beard, when bound on a bat,
Instructed his wife on the key of a flat!

Blue-Beard, the Monday following,
His jealous feeling swallowing,
  Packed all his clothes together
    In a leather-
      Bound valise,
And, feigning reprehensibly,
He started out, ostensibly
  By traveling to learn a
    Bit of Smyrna
      And of Greece.

His wife made but a cursory
Inspection of the nursery;
  The kitchen and the airy
    Little dairy
      Were a bore,
As well as big or scanty rooms,
And billiard, bath, and ante-rooms,
  But not that interdicted
    And restricted
      Little door!

For, all her curiosity
Awakened by the closet he
  So carefully had hidden,
    And forbidden
      Her to see,
This damsel disobedient
Did something inexpedient,
  And in the keyhole tiny
    Turned the shiny
      Little key:

Then started back impulsively,
And shrieked aloud convulsively—
  Three heads of girls he'd wedded
    And beheaded
      Met her eye!
And turning round, much terrified,
Her darkest fears were verified,
  For Blue-Beard stood behind her,
    Come to find her
      On the sly!

Perceiving she was fated to
Be soon decapitated, too,
  She telegraphed her brothers
    And some others
      What she feared.
        And Sister Anne looked out for them,

In readiness to shout for them
  Whenever in the distance
    With assistance
      They appeared.

But only from her battlement
She saw some dust that cattle meant.
   The ordinary story
     Isn't gory,
       But a jest.
But here's the truth unqualified.
The husband *wasn't* mollified
   Her head is in his bloody
     Little study
       With the rest!

The Moral: Wives, we must allow,
Who to their husbands will not bow,
A stern and dreadful lesson learn
When, as you've read, they're cut in turn.

*How Rumplestilz Held Out
in Vain for a Bonus*

In Germany there lived an earl
 Who had a charming niece:
And never gave the timid girl
 A single moment's peace!
Whatever low and menial task
 His fancy flitted through,

He did not hesitate to ask
   That shrinking child to do.
(I see with truly honest shame you
   Are blushing, and I do not blame you.
A tale like this the feelings softens,
   And brings the tears, as does "Two Orphans.")

She had to wash the windows, and
   She had to scrub the floors,
She had to lend a willing hand
   To fifty other chores:
She gave the dog his exercise,
   She read the earl the news,
She ironed all his evening ties,
   And polished all his shoes,
She cleaned the tins that filled the dairy,
   She cut the claws of the canary,
And then, at night, with manner winsome,
   When coal was wanted, carried in some!

But though these tasks were quite enough,
   He thought them all too few,
And so her uncle, rude and rough,
   Invented something new.
He took her to a little room,
   Her willingness to tax,
And pointed out a broken loom
   And half a ton of flax,
Observing: "Spin six pairs of trousers!"
   His haughty manner seemed to rouse hers.
She met his scornful glances proudly—
   And for an answer whistled loudly!

But when the earl went down the stair
   She yielded to her fears.

Gave way at last to grim despair,
   And melted into tears:
When suddenly, from out the wall,
   As if he felt at home,
There pounced a singularly small
   And much distorted gnome.
He smiled a smile extremely vapid,
   And set to work in fashion rapid;
No time for resting he deducted,
   And soon the trousers were constructed.

The girl observed: "How very nice
    To help me out this way!"
The gnome replied: "A certain price
    Of course you'll have to pay.
I'll call to-morrow afternoon,
    My due reward to claim,
And then you'll sing another tune
    Unless you guess my name!"
He indicated with a gesture
The pile of newly fashioned vesture:
His eyes on hers a moment centered,
And then he went, as he had entered.

R-r-r-r-rumplestilz!

As by this tale you have been grieved
   And heartily distressed,
Kind sir, you will be much relieved
   To know his name she guessed:
But if I do not tell the same,
   Pray count it not a crime:—
I've tried my best, and for that name
   I can't find any rhyme!
Yet spare me from remarks injurious:
   I will not leave you foiled and furious.
If something must proclaim the answer,
   And I cannot, the title can, sir!

The Moral is: All said and done,
There's nothing new beneath the sun,
And many times before, a title
Was incapacity's requital!

How Jack Made the Giants
Uncommonly Sore

Of all the ill-fated
Boys ever created
   Young Jack was the wretchedest lad:
An emphatic, erratic,
Dogmatic fanatic
   Was foisted upon him as dad!
From the time he could walk,
And before he could talk,
   His wearisome training began,
On a highly barbarian,
Disciplinarian,
Nearly Tartarean
        Plan!

He taught him some Raleigh,
And some of Macaulay,
   Till all of "Horatius" he knew,
And the drastic, sarcastic,
Fantastic, scholastic
   Philippics of "Junius," too.
He made him learn lots
Of the poems of Watts,
   And frequently said he ignored,
On principle, any son's

Title to benisons
Till he'd learned Tennyson's
        "Maud."

"For these are the giants
Of thought and of science,"
  He said in his positive way:
"So weigh them, obey them,
Display them, and lay them
  To heart in your infancy's day!"
Jack made no reply,
But he said on the sly
  An eloquent word, that had come
From a quite indefensible,

Most reprehensible,
But indispensable
      Chum.

By the time he was twenty
Jack had such a plenty
  Of books and paternal advice,
Though seedy and needy,
Indeed he was greedy
  For vengeance, whatever the price!
In the editor's seat
Of a critical sheet
He found the revenge that he sought;
And, with sterling appliance of
Mind, wrote defiance of
All of the giants of
      Thought.

He'd thunder and grumble
At high and at humble
  Until he became, in a while,
Mordacious, pugnacious,
Rapacious. Good gracious!
  They called him the Yankee Carlyle!

But he never took rest
On his quarrelsome quest
Of the giants, both mighty and small.
He slated, distorted them,
Hanged them and quartered them,
Till he had slaughtered them
        All.

And this is *The Moral* that lies in the verse:
If you have a go farther, you're apt to fare worse.
(When you turn it around it is different rather:—
You're not apt to go worse if you have a fair father!)

How Rudeness and Kindness
Were Justly Rewarded

Once on a time, long years ago
   (Just when I quite forget),
Two maidens lived beside the Po,
   One blonde and one brunette.
The blonde one's character was mild,
From morning until night she smiled,
Whereas the one whose hair was brown
Did little else than pine and frown.
   (*I* think one ought to draw the line
   At girls who always frown and pine!)

The blonde one learned to play the harp,
   Like all accomplished dames,
And trained her voice to take *C* sharp
   As well as Emma Eames;
Made baskets out of scented grass,
And paper-weights of hammered brass,
And lots of other odds and ends
For gentleman and lady friends.
   (*I* think it takes a deal of sense
   To manufacture gifts for gents!)

The dark one wore an air of gloom,
   Proclaimed the world a bore,
And took her breakfast in her room
   Three mornings out of four.
With crankiness she seemed imbued,
And everything she said was rude:
She sniffed, and sneered, and, what is more,
When very much provoked, she swore!
   (*I* think that I could never care

For any girl who'd learned to swear!)

One day the blonde was striding past
  A forest, all alone,
When all at once her eyes she cast
  Upon a wrinkled crone,
Who tottered near with shaking knees,
And said: "A penny, if you please!"
And you will learn with some surprise
This was a fairy in disguise!
  (*I* think it must be hard to know
  A fairy who's incognito!)

The maiden filled her trembling palms
  With coinage of the realm.
The fairy said: "Take back your alms!
  My heart they overwhelm.
Henceforth at every word shall slip
A pearl or ruby from your lip!"
And, when the girl got home that night, —
 She found the fairy's words were right!
  (*I* think there are not many girls
  Whose words are worth their weight in pearls!)

It happened that the cross brunette,
  Ten minutes later, came
Along the self-same road, and met
  That bent and wrinkled dame,
Who asked her humbly for a sou.
The girl replied: "Get out with you!"
The fairy cried: "Each word you drop,
A toad from out your mouth shall hop!"
  (*I* think that nothing incommodes
  One's speech like uninvited toads!)

This shows why each suitor, who rode up to spark,
Would mark the toad maybe, but ne'er toed the mark.

And so it was, the cheerful blonde
   Lived on in joy and bliss,
And grew pecunious, beyond
   The dreams of avarice!
And to a nice young man was wed,
And I have often heard it said
No other man who ever walked
Most loved his wife when most she talked!
   (*I* think this very fact, forsooth,
   Goes far to prove I tell the truth!)
The cross brunette the fairy's joke
   By hook or crook survived,
But still at every word she spoke
   An ugly toad arrived,

Until at last she had to come
To feigning she was wholly dumb,
Whereat the suitors swarmed around,
And soon a wealthy mate she found.
  (*I* think nobody ever knew
  The happier husband of the two!)

The Moral of the tale is: Bah!
Nous avons changé tout celà.
No clear idea I hope to strike
Of what *your* nicest girl is like,
But she whose best young man *I* am
Is not an oyster, nor a clam!

How Beauty Contrived to Get
Square with the Beast

Miss Guinevere Platt
Was so beautiful that
   She couldn't remember the day
When one of her swains
Hadn't taken the pains
   To send her a mammoth bouquet.
And the postman had found,
On the whole of his round,
   That no one received such a lot
Of bulky epistles
As, waiting his whistles,
   The beautiful Guinevere got!

A significant sign
That her charm was divine
   Was seen in society, when
The chaperons sniffed
With their eyebrows alift:
   "Whatever's got into the men?"
There was always a man
Who was holding her fan,
   And twenty that danced in details,
And a couple of mourners,
Who brooded in corners,
   And gnawed their mustaches and nails.

John Jeremy Platt
Wouldn't stay in the flat,
　　For his beautiful daughter he missed:
When he'd taken his tub,
He would hie to his club,
　　And dally with poker or whist.
At the end of a year
It was perfectly clear
　　That he'd never computed the cost,
For he hadn't a penny

To settle the many
Ten thousands of dollars he'd lost!

F. Ferdinand Fife
Was a student of life:
　He was coarse, and excessively fat,
With a beard like a goat's,
But he held all the notes
　Of ruined John Jeremy Platt!
With an adamant smile
That was brimming with guile,
　He said: "I am took with the face
Of your beautiful daughter,
And wed me she ought ter,
　To save you from utter disgrace!"

Miss Guinevere Platt
Didn't hesitate at
　Her duty's imperative call.
When they looked at the bride
All the chaperons cried:
　"She isn't so bad, after all!"
Of the desolate men
There were something like ten
　Who took up political lives,
And the flower of the flock
Went and fell off a dock,
　And the rest married hideous wives!

But the beautiful wife
Of F. Ferdinand Fife
　Was the wildest that ever was known:
She'd grumble and glare,
Till the man didn't dare
　To say that his soul was his own.
She sneered at his ills,
And quadrupled his bills,
And spent nearly twice what he earned;
Her husband deserted,
　And frivoled, and flirted,
Till Ferdinand's reason was turned.

This shows how at poker one loses his pelf
When the other's a joker and knave in himself.

He repented too late,
And his terrible fate
  Upon him so heavily sat,
That he swore at the day
When he sat down to play
  At cards with John Jeremy Platt.
He was dead in a year,
And the fair Guinevere

In society sparkled again,
While the chaperons fluttered
Their fans, as they muttered:
   "She's getting exceedingly plain!"

The Moral: Predicaments often are found
That beautiful duty is apt to get round:
But greedy extortioners better beware
For dutiful beauty is apt to get square!

How a Fair One no Hope to
His Highness Accorded

She has slid down the channels
Of history's annals
  Disguised as the child of a king,
But that is a glib
And iniquitous fib,
  For she never was any such thing:
They called her the Fair One with Golden Locks,
And it's true she had lovers who swarmed in
        flocks,
But the rest is ironic;
Her business chronic
Was selling hair-tonic
        By bottle and box!

From the dawn till the gloaming
She used to sit combing
      Her hair in a languorous way.
And her suitors would stop
To look into the shop,
      And stand there the rest of the day.
She filled them with mute, but with deep despair,
For she never glanced up, with a smile, to where
They stood about, crushing

Each other, and blushing:
She simply kept brushing
        Her beautiful hair.
 But a prince who was passing,
Engaged in amassing
  Some facts on American life,
Was suddenly struck

54

By the fact that his luck
   Might give him that girl for a wife!
His rashness he didn't attempt to excuse,
He entered the shop and he stated his views.
Remarking,
         "My jewel,
I'm confident you will
Not wish to be cruel
        Enough to refuse.

"Most winsome of creatures,"
He told her, "your features
   Have led me to candidly say
That no other beside
Would I have for a bride:
   We'll be married a week from to-day!
I belong to a long and a titled line,
And the least of your wishes I won't decline;
Next month I will usher
My wife into Russia:—
Sweet comber and brusher,
        Consider you're mine!"

She looked at him squarely,
Considered him fairly,
   Her glance was as keen as a knife,

Then she turned up her nose,
And, with icy repose,
　　She answered: "Well, not on your life!
You're not on the paper the only blot!
Do you think I come twelve in a parcel—what?
Me pose as your dearie?
Oh, go and chase Peary!
You're making me weary.
　　　　　　　　Now git!"

　　(He got!)

The crowd that had waited
Outside was elated
　　So much by the prince's mischance,
That they greeted with jeers
And ironical cheers,
　　The end of his little romance.
They said: "Did it hurt when the ground you hit?"
They searched for some mark where the prince
　　　　　　had lit,
And as he looked colder,
They only grew bolder,
And tapped on his shoulder
　　　　　　　　With: "Tag! You're It!"

The lengthy discussion
That sensitive Russian
　　Compiled on the U. S. A.
Was read by the maid,
As she carelessly played
　　With her beautiful hair one day.
"The talk you hear in that primitive land,"
He wrote, "nobody can understand."
"Somebody who guffed him,"
She said, "has stuffed him,
And easily bluffed him
　　　　　　　　To beat the band!"

This shows how, with never a shadow of doubt,
When you go in for love you are apt to come out.

The Moral: The people across the brine
Are exceedingly strong on Auld Lang Syne,
But they're lost in the push when they strike a
      gang
That is strong on American new line slang!

]*How Thomas a Maid from
a Dragon Released*

Though Philip the Second
Of France was reckoned
  No coward, his breath came short
When they told him a dragon
As big as a wagon
  Was waiting below in the court!
A dragon so long, and so wide, and so fat,
That he couldn't get in at the door to chat:
The king couldn't leave him
Outside and grieve him,
He had to receive him
                Upon the mat,

The dragon bowed nicely,
And very concisely
  He stated the reason he'd called:
He made the disclosure
With frigid composure.
  King Philip was simply appalled!
He demanded for eating, a fortnight apart,
The monarch's ten daughters, all dear to his heart.

"And now you'll produce," he
Concluded, "the juicy
And succulent Lucie
   By way of start!"

King Philip was pliant,
And far from defiant
 —"And servile," no doubt you retort!—
But if *you* struck a snag on
A bottle-green dragon,
 Who filled up two-thirds of your court,
And curled up his tail on your new tin roof,
And made your piazza groan under his hoof,
Would you threaten and thunder,
Or just knuckle under
Completely, I wonder,
   If put to proof?

By way of a truce, he
Brought out little Lucie
 And watched her conducted away,
But all of the others
Were out with their brothers!
 Thus gaining a little delay,
He promised through heralds sent west and east,
His crown, and his kingdom, and last, not least,
His daughter so sightly

To any one knightly
Who'd come and politely
   Wipe out that beast!

For love of the charmer,
Arrayed in his armor,
 Each suitor for glory who yearned,
Would gallantly hasten,
The dragon to chasten,
 But none of them ever returned!
When the dragon had eaten some sixteen score
He hung up this sign on his cavern door,
Whereat he lay pronely
In majesty lonely:

   There's Standing Room Only
   For Three Knights
     More!

A slim adolescent,
His beard only crescent,
 Rode up at this stage of the game
To where the old sinner
Lay gorged with his dinner,
 And breathing out torrents of flame.
He gathered a tip from the flaunting sign,
And took his position the fourth in line,
Until, as foreboded,
By food incommoded,
The dragon exploded
   At half-past nine.

The king was delighted
At first when he sighted
 The victor, but then in dismay
Regretted his promise.
The stripling was Thomas,
 His Majesty's *valet-de-pied*!

This shows how a servant may laugh at the Fates,
Since everything comes to the fellow who waits.

He asked him at once: "Will you compromise?"
But Thomas looked straight in his master's eyes,
And answered severely:
"I see your game clearly,
And scorn it sincerely.
                    Hand out the prize!"

Not long did he linger
Before on the finger
    Of Lucie he fitted a ring:
A month or two later
They made him dictator,
    In place of the elderly king:
He was lauded by pulpit, and boomed by press,
And no one had ever a chance to guess,
Beholding this hero
Who ruled like a Nero,
His valor was zero,
                    Or something less.

The Moral: And still from Nice to Calais
Discretion's the better part of—
                    —*valets!*

How a Beauty was Waked
and Her Suitor was Suited

Albeit wholly penniless,
Prince Charming wasn't any less
    Conceited than a Croesus or a modern
        millionaire:
Though often in necessity,
No one would ever guess it. He
    Was candidly insolvent, and he frankly didn't
        care!
Of the many debts he made
Not a one was ever paid,
    But no one ever pressed him to refund the
        borrowed gold:
While he recklessly kept spending,
People gladly kept on lending,
For the fact they knew a title
                Was requital
                Twenty-fold!
(He lived in sixteen sixty-three,
    This smooth unblushing article,
Since when, as far as I can see,
    Men haven't changed a particle!)

In Charming's principality
There was a wild locality,
    Composed of sombre forest, and of steep and
        frowning crags,
Of pheasant and of rabbit, too;
And here it was his habit to
    Go hunting with his courtiers in the keen pursuit
        of stags.
But the charger that he rode
So mercurially strode

That the prince on one occasion left the others in
the lurch,
And the falling darkness found him,
With no vassals left around him,
 Near a building like an abbey,
  Or a shabby
  Ruined church.
His Highness said: "I'll ring the bell
 And stay till morning in it!" (He
Took Hobson's choice, for no hotel
 There was in the vicinity.)

His ringing was so vehement
That any one could see he meant
 To suffer no refusal, but, in spite of all the din,
There was no answer audible,
And so, with courage laudable,
 His Royal Highness turned the knob, and stoutly
  entered in.
Then he strode across the court,
But he suddenly stopped short
 When he passed within the castle by a massive
  oaken door:
There were courtiers without number,
But they all were plunged in slumber,
The prince's ear delighting
  By uniting
  In a snore.
The prince remarked: "This must be Philadelphia,
 Pennsylvania!"
(And so was born the jest that's still
The comic journal's mania!)

This shows how the prince won the princess's heart,
And the end of her sleeping was simply a start.

With torpor reprehensible,
Numb, comatose, insensible,
   The flunkeys and the chamberlains all slumbered like the
   dead,
And snored so loud and mournfully,
That Charming passed them scornfully
   And came to where a princess lay asleep upon a
        bed.
She was so extremely fair
That His Highness didn't care
   For the risk, and so he kissed her ere a single
        word he spoke:—
In a jiffy maids and pages,
Ushers, lackeys, squires, and sages,
   As fresh as if they'd been at least
          A week awake,

      Awoke,
And hastened, bustled, dashed and ran
   Up stairways and through galleries:
In brief, they one and all began
   Again to earn their salaries!

Aroused from her paralysis,
As if in deep analysis
   Of him who had awakened her, the princess met
       his eye:
Her glance at first was critical,
And sternly analytical.
   And then she dropped her lashes and she gave a
       little sigh.
As he watched her, wholly dumb,
She observed: "You doubtless come

For one of two good reasons, and I'm going to
    ask you which.
Do you mean my house to harry, Or do you propose to
    marry?"
  He answered: "I may rue it,
    But I'll do it,
      If you're rich!"
The princess murmured with a smile:
  "I've millions, at the least, to come!"
The prince cried: "Please excuse me, while
  I go and get the priest to come!"

The Moral: When affairs go ill
The sleeping partner foots the bill.

How Jack Found that Beans
May go Back on a Chap

Without the slightest basis
For hypochondriasis
   A widow had forebodings which a cloud around her
   flung,
And with expression cynical
For half the day a clinical
   Thermometer she held beneath her tongue.

Whene'er she read the papers
She suffered from the vapors,
   At every tale of malady or accident she'd groan;
In every new and smart disease,
From housemaid's knee to heart disease,
   She recognized the symptoms as her own!

She had a yearning chronic
To try each novel tonic,
   Elixir, panacea, lotion, opiate, and balm;
And from a homœopathist
Would change to an hydropathist,
   And back again, with stupefying calm!

The closets of her villa
Were full of sarsaparilla,
   Ammonia, digitalis, bronchial troches, soda
       mint.
Restoratives hirsutical,
And soaps to clean the cuticle,
   And iodine, and peptonoids, and lint.

She was nervous, cataleptic,
And anemic, and dyspeptic:
   Though not convinced of apoplexy, yet she had
       her fears.
She dwelt with force fanatical
Upon a twinge rheumatical,
   And said she had a buzzing in her ears!

Now all of this bemoaning And this grumbling
       and this groaning
   The mind of Jack, her son and heir,
       unconscionably bored.
His heart completely hardening, He gave his time
       to gardening,
   For raising beans was something he adored.

Each hour in accents morbid
This limp maternal bore bid
   Her callous son affectionate and lachrymose
       good-bys.
She never granted Jack a day
Without some long "Alackaday!"

Accompanied by rolling of the eyes.

But Jack, no panic showing,
Just watched his beanstalk growing,
    And twined with tender fingers the tendrils up
        the pole.
At all her words funereal
He smiled a smile ethereal,
    Or sighed an absent-minded "Bless my soul!"

That hollow-hearted creature
Would never change a feature:
    No tear bedimmed his eye, however touching
        was her talk.
She never fussed or flurried him,
The only thing that worried him
    Was when no bean-pods grew upon the stalk!

But then he wabbled loosely His head, and wept
      profusely,

And, taking out his handkerchief to mop away his
  tears,
Exclaimed: "It hasn't got any!"
He found this blow to botany
  Was sadder than were all his mother's fears.

The Moral is that gardeners pine
Whene'er no pods adorn the vine.
Of all sad words experience gleans
The saddest are: "It *might* have beans."
  (I did not make this up myself:
  'Twas in a book upon my shelf.
  It's witty, but I don't deny
  It's rather Whittier than I!)

How a Cat Was Annoyed and
a Poet Was Booted

A poet had a cat.
There is nothing odd in that—
    (I *might* make a little pun about the *Mews!*)
But what is really more
Remarkable, she wore
    A pair of pointed patent-leather shoes.
        And I doubt me greatly whether
            E'er you heard the like of that:
Pointed shoes of patent-leather
                On a cat!

His time he used to pass
Writing sonnets, on the grass—
    (I *might* say something good on *pen* and *sward!*)
While the cat sat near at hand,
Trying hard to understand
    The poems he occasionally roared.
        (I myself possess a feline,

But when poetry I roar
He is sure to make a bee-line
  For the door.)

The poet, cent by cent,
All his patrimony spent—
 (I *might* tell how he went from *werse* to *werse!*)
Till the cat was sure she could,
By advising, do him good
 So addressed him in a manner that was terse:
  "We are bound toward the scuppers,
   And the time has come to act,
Or we'll both be on our uppers
  For a fact!"

On her boot she fixed her eye,
But the boot made no reply—
 (I *might* say: "Couldn't speak to save *its sole!*")
And the foolish bard, instead
Of responding, only read
 A verse that wasn't bad upon the whole:
  And it pleased the cat so greatly,
   Though she knew not what it meant,
That I'll quote approximately
  How it went:—

"If I should live to be
The last leaf upon the tree"—
 (I *might* put in: "I think I'd just as *leaf!*")
"Let them smile, as I do now,
At the old forsaken bough"—
 Well, he'd plagiarized it bodily, in brief!
  But that cat of simple breeding
   Couldn't read the lines between,
So she took it to a leading
  Magazine.

She was jarred and very sore
When they showed her to the door.
    (I *might* hit off the *door* that was *a jar*!)
To the spot she swift returned
Where the poet sighed and yearned,
    And she told him that he'd gone a little far.
      "Your performance with this rhyme has
        Made me absolutely sick,"
She remarked. "I think the time has
        Come to kick!"

I could fill up half the page
With descriptions of her rage—
    (I *might* say that she went a bit *too fur*!)
When he smiled and murmured: "Shoo!"
"There is one thing I can do!"
    She answered with a wrathful kind of purr.
      "You may shoo me, and it suit you,
        But I feel my conscience bid
Me, as tit for tat, to boot you!"

(Which she did.)

The Moral of the plot
(Though I say it, as should not!)
Is: An editor is difficult to suit.
But again there're other times
When the man who fashions rhymes
Is a rascal, and a bully one to boot!

How Much Fortunatus Could
Do with a Cap

Fortunatus, a fisherman Dane,
Set out on a sudden for Spain,
  Because, runs the story,
  He'd met with a hoary
        Mysterious sorcerer chap,
Who, trouble to save him,
Most thoughtfully gave him
        A magical traveling cap.
I barely believe that the story is true,
But here's what that cap was reported to do.

Suppose you were sitting at home,
And you wished to see Paris or Rome,
  You'd pick up that bonnet,
  You'd carefully don it,
        The name of the city you'd call,

And the very next minute
By Jove, you were in it,
      Without having started at all!
One moment you sauntered on upper Broadway,
And the next on the Corso or rue de la Paix!

Why, it beat every journey of Cook's,
Knocked spots out of Baedeker's books!
  He stepped from his doorway
  Direct into Norway,
      He hopped in a trice to Ceylon,
He saw Madagascar,
Went round by Alaska,
      And called on a girl in Luzon:
If they said she'd be down in a moment or two,
He took, while he waited, a peek at Peru!

He could wake up at eight in Siam,
Take his tub, if he wanted, in Guam.
  Eat breakfast in Kansas,
  And lunch in Matanzas,
      Go out for a walk in Brazil,
Take tea in Madeira,
Dine on the Riviera,
      And smoke his cigar in Seville,
Go out to the theatre in Vladivostok,
And retire in New York at eleven o'clock!

Every tongue he could readily speak:
French, German, Italian, Greek,
  Norwegian, Bulgarian,
  Turkish, Bavarian,
      Japanese, Hindustanee,
Russian and Mexican!
He was a lexicon,
      Such as you seldom will see.
His knowledge linguistic gave Ollendorff fits,
And brought a hot flush to the face of Berlitz!

This shows Fortunatus, a restlessness feeling,
Forsaking his fishing, and leaving his ceiling.

He would bow in an intimate way
To Menelik and to Loubet,
  He was frequently beckoned,
  By William the Second,
    A word of advice to receive,
He talked with bravado
About the Mikado,
    King Oscar, Oom Paul, the Khedive,
King Victor Emmanuel Second, the Shah,
King Edward the Seventh, Kwang Su, and the
    Czar!

But what did he get from it all?
His wife used to wait in the hall!

When this wandering mortal
Set foot on the portal,
  She always appeared on the scene,
And, far from ideally,
Remarked: "Well, I *really*
  Would like to know where you have been!"

She'd indulge in a copious cry,
She'd remark she'd undoubtedly die,
  Or, like many another,
  Go back to her mother,
   And what would the world think of *that*?
She only grew pleasant,
When offered a present
   Of gloves or a gown or a hat:
And more than his talisman saved him in fare
Fortunatus expended in putting things square!

Now what is the good of a wandering life,
If you have to tell all that you do to your wife?

And *The Moral* is easily said:
Like our hero, you're certain to find,
When such a cap goes on a head,
Retribution will follow behind!

How a Princess Was Wooed
from Habitual Sadness

In days of old the King of Saxe
  Had singular opinions,
For with a weighty battle-axe
  He brutalized his minions,
And, when he'd nothing to employ
  His mind, he chose a village,
And with an air of savage joy
  Delivered it to pillage.

But what aroused within his breast
  A rage well-nigh primeval
Was, most of all, his daughter, dressed
  In fashion mediæval:
The gowns that pleased this maiden's eye
  Were simple as Utopia,
And for a hat she had a high
  Inverted cornucopia.

In all her life she'd never smiled,
  Her sadness was abysmal:
The boisterous monarch found his child
  Unutterably dismal.
He therefore said the prince who made
  Her laughter from its shell come,
Besides in ducats being paid,
  Might wed the girl, and welcome!
I ought to say, ere I forget,
  She was uncommon comely—
(Who ever read a Grimm tale yet,
  In which the girl was homely?)
And so the King's announcement drew

Nine princes in a column.
But all in vain. The princess grew,
If anything, more solemn.

One read her "Innocents Abroad,"
The next wore clothes eccentric,
The third one swallowed half his sword,
As in the circus-tent trick.
Thus eight of them into her cool
Reserve but deeper shoved her:
There was but one authentic fool—
The prince who really loved her!

He'd alternate between the height
  Of hope and deep abasement,
He caught distressing colds at night,
  By watching 'neath her casement:
He did what I have done, I know,
  And you, I do not doubt it,—
Instead of bottling up his woe,
  He bored his friends about it!

In brooding on the ways of Fate
  Long hours he daily wasted,
His food remained upon his plate,
  'Twas scarcely touched or tasted:
He said the bitter things of love,
  All lovers, save a few, say,
And learned by heart the verses of
  Swinburne, and A. de Musset!

This attitude his wished-for bride
  To silent laughter goaded,
Until he talked of suicide,
  And then the girl exploded!
"You make me laugh, and so," she said,
  "I'll marry you next season."
(Not half the people who are wed
  Have half so good a reason!)

The Moral: The deliberate clown
Can never beat love's barriers down:
'Tis better to be like the owl,
Comic because so grave a fowl.
From him we well may take our cue—
By him be taught, to wit, to woo!

How a Girl was too Reckless
of Grammar by Far

Matilda Maud Mackenzie frankly hadn't any chin,
Her hands were rough, her feet she turned
        invariably in;
    Her general form was German,
        By which I mean that you
    Her waist could not determine
        To within a foot or two:
And not only did she stammer,
But she used the kind of grammar
    That is called, for sake of euphony, askew.

From what I say about her, don't imagine I desire
A prejudice against this worthy creature to inspire.
    She was willing, she was active,
        She was sober, she was kind,
    But she *never* looked attractive
        And she *hadn't* any mind!
I knew her more than slightly,
And I treated her politely
        When I met her, but of course I wasn't
            blind!

Matilda Maud Mackenzie had a habit that was
        droll,
She spent her morning seated on a rock or on a
        knoll,
    And threw with much composure
        A smallish rubber ball

At an inoffensive osier
  By a little waterfall;
  But Matilda's way of throwing
  Was like other people's mowing,
    And she never hit the willow-tree at all!

This serves in the easiest way to explain
  What is meant by taking an aim in vain.
One day as Miss Mackenzie with uncommon
    ardor tried
To hit the mark, the missile flew exceptionally
    wide,

And, before her eyes astounded,
   On a fallen maple's trunk
Ricochetted, and rebounded
   In the rivulet, and sunk!
Matilda, greatly frightened,
In her grammar unenlightened,
      Remarked: "Well now I ast yer! Who'd 'er
         thunk?"

But what a marvel followed! From the pool at once
      there rose
A frog, the sphere of rubber balanced deftly on his
      nose.
   He beheld her fright and frenzy,
     And, her panic to dispel,
   On his knee by Miss Mackenzie
    He obsequiously fell.
With quite as much decorum
As a speaker in a forum
     He started in his history to tell.

"Fair maid," he said, "I beg you, do not hesitate or
      wince,
If you'll promise that you'll wed me, I'll at once
      become a prince;
   For a fairy old and vicious
    An enchantment round me spun!"
   Then he looked up, unsuspicious,
    And he saw what he had won,
And in terms of sad reproach he
Made some comments, *sotto voce*,*

     * (Which the publishers have bidden me to
      shun!)

Matilda Maud Mackenzie said, as if she meant to
 scold:
"I *never*! Why, you forward thing! Now ain't you
 awful bold!"
  Just a glance he paused to give her,
    And his head was seen to clutch,
  Then he darted to the river,
    And he dived to beat the Dutch!
While the wrathful maiden panted:
"I don't think he was enchanted!"
      (And he really didn't look it overmuch!)

90

The Moral: In one's language one conservative
         should be:
Speech is silver, and it never should be free!

How the Peaceful Aladdin
Gave Way to His Madness

His name was Aladdin.
The clothes he was clad in
  Proclaimed him an Arab at sight,
And he had for a chum

Grimm Tales Made Gay

An uncommonly rum
   Old afreet, six cubits in height.
This person infernal,
Who seemed so fraternal,
   At bottom was frankly a scamp:
His future to sadden,
He gave to Aladdin
   A wonderful magical lamp.

 A marvel he dubbed it.
He said if one rubbed it
   One's wishes were done on the spot.
Now what would you do
Were it offered to you?
   Refuse it undoubtedly (not)!
It's thus comprehensive
With pleasure extensive
Aladdin accepted the gift,
   And, by it befriended,
Erected a splendid
Château, with a bath and a lift!

Not dreaming of malice,
One year in his palace
   He led a luxurious life,
Till his genius dread
Put it into his head
   That he needed a beautiful wife.
Responding to friction,
The lamp this affliction
   At once for Aladdin secured;
The latter, delighted,
Imagined he sighted
A future of quiet assured.

When gladly he chose her,
He didn't suppose her
   A philatelist, always agape

For novelties, yet
She had all of the set
   Of triangular stamps of the Cape.
Some people malicious
Proclaimed her Mauritius
   One-penny vermilion a sell.
But that was all rot. It
Was true she had got it,
   And the tuppenny blue one as well!

Since thus she collected,
As might be expected,
   She didn't for *bric-à-brac* care,
So she traded the lamp
For an Ecuador stamp
   That somebody told her was rare!
This act served to madden
The mind of Aladdin,
   But, 'spite of his impotent wrath,
His manor-house vanished,
To nothingness banished,
   And while he was taking a bath!

The average Arab
Is hard as a scarab
   When some one has wounded his pride,
So he jumped up and down,
With a cynical frown,
   On the *face* of his beautiful bride!
He had picked up a cargo
Of curious *argot*
   While living in Paris the gay;
In the slang of that city
He cried without pity:
   "*Comme ça tu me fich'ras la paix!*"

Grimm Tales Made Gay

The Moral: When stamps you're adept on
Of risks you are reckless, and yet
Beware! If your face is once stepped on,
   That's the last stamp you're likely to get!

How a Fisherman Corked
up His Foe in a Jar

A fisherman lived on the shore,
  (It's a habit that fishers affect,)
And his life was a hideous bore:
  He had nothing to do but collect
Continual harvests of seaweed and shells,
  Which he stuck upon photograph frames,
To sell to the guests in the summer hotels
  With the quite inappropriate names!

He would wander along by the edge
  Of the sea, and I know for a fact
From the pools with a portable dredge
  He would curious creatures extract:
And, during the season, he always took lots
  Of tourists out fishing for bass,

And showed them politely impossible spots,
  In the culpable way of his class.

It happened one day, as afar
  He roved on the glistening strand,
That he chanced on a curious jar,
  Which lay on a hummock of sand.
It was closed at the mouth with a cork and a seal,
  And over the top there was tied
A cloth, and the fisherman couldn't but feel
  That he ought to see what was inside.

But what were his fear and surprise
  When the stopper he held in his hand!
For a genie of singular size
  Appeared in a trice on the sand,
Who said in the roughest and rudest of tones:
  "A monster you've foolishly freed!
I shall simply make way with you, body and
      bones,
And that with phenomenal speed!"

This shows us the fisher beginning to blow
Of preserving himself while he pickled his foe.

The fisherman looked in his face,
    And answered him boldly: "My friend,
How you ever were packed in that space
    Is something I don't comprehend.
Pray do me the favor to show me how you
    Can do it, as large as you are."
The genie retorted: "That's just what I'll do!"
And promptly reëntered the jar.

The fisherman corked him up tight:
    The genie protested and raved,
But for all he accomplished, he might
    As well all his shouting have saved.
And, whenever a generous bonus is paid,
    The fisherman willingly tells
The singular tale of this trick that he played,
To the guests in the summer hotels.

The Moral: When fortune you strike,
And you've slipped through a dangerous crack,
Get as forward as ever you like,
But never, oh, *never* get back!

Envoi

Now don't go and say you'd a
    dim
Idea of these stories before,
For I've frankly confessed
    them from Grimm,
The monarch of magical lore:

And if, by repeating, I took
Your time, I will candidly
    vow
This moral (the last in the
    book)
Has never been published till
    now!

The Moral: The skeleton's Grimm,
  But I have supplied the apparel,
So it's fifty per cent, of it Him,
  And it's fifty per cent. of it Carryl.

But still (from the personal severing,
  For it isn't my nature to grump,)
I acknowledge a measure of Levering
  Levering-ed the whole of the lump!

Lightning Source UK Ltd.
Milton Keynes UK
UKOW04f2140161213

223136UK00001B/285/A